Table of Contents
The Essential Guide to the ADI Part 3 Test

National Standard for driver and rider training (NSDRT)   Back of the book

Introduction

The format of the ADI Part 3 Test changes during October 2017. The 'old style' role-play test will no longer be used to test instructional ability.

Now, instead of the DVSA Examiner role-playing a pupil, the test candidate will be required to supply their own 'learner'. They will have to carry out a 'client centred' training session / lesson which the Examiner will watch and grade from the back seat.

Why have the DVSA changed the test?

The industry has confirmed that the current role-play ADI part 3 test, which relies on pre-set tests, is both unrealistic and restrictive. It doesn't give trainee instructors enough opportunity to demonstrate the full range of skills that will they need when qualified.

The change will mean that new ADIs won't need to undertake additional training or learn different teaching methods ahead of their standards check.

It will also enable the test to be delivered at a greater number of test centres, and local to where their training has taken place.

This book will explain **HOW** the test is carried out and **WHAT** the examiner is looking for. You will find clear and simple advice on:

- The format of the test
- The type of learner you can take
- The type of lesson you should carry out
- How to prepare for the test

The book alone cannot guarantee success, you will also need:

- A good training provider
- Structured training
- Commitment
- Determination

At the back of the book we have included the National Standard for Driver and Rider Training (NSDRT) – it's imperative that you read this document; the advice contained within will help you to understand the new competence framework.

Good luck!

Let's start by looking at what the ADI Part 3 Test is...

The aim of the ADI part 3 test is to check your ability to instruct, and whether your instructional techniques are helping a person to learn in an effective way.

Simply put - it is a test of your ability, as a potential driving instructor (PDI), to teach and pass on your knowledge to a pupil. At the end of the test, your 'pupil' ***must*** go away having learnt, practiced and improved new and existing skills.

Format of the test

All ADI part 3 tests must be conducted in either English or Welsh.

The Examiner will observe you giving a 1 hour lesson to your pupil. They will assess the instruction that you deliver to the pupil based on the ADI Part 3 (SC) form (you will find this form on ***page 8***) and on the National Standard for Driver and Rider Training (included at the back of this book).

Types of Part 3 test lesson pupil scenarios

There are several different types of pupil that the test candidate can supply for the Part 3 Test lesson, they are any of the following scenarios:

- Partly trained or inexperienced learner
- Experienced pupil, close to test standard
- Full Licence Holder – new
- Experienced Full Licence Holder

There is more information on lesson scenarios starting on ***page 11***....

*Note: Classroom sessions and 'off road' lessons are **NOT** allowed for the test.*

Test Route

Because you, the PDI, are responsible for the lesson, you must have good knowledge of the area around the test centre.

This is so you can:

- Plan the lesson
- Give directions to the pupil in good time

> As your test day approaches, it's a good idea to drive around the roads near the test centre in order to familiarise yourself with them. This will help you plan the lesson and should also elliminate any surprises or confusion on the day, enabling you to concentrate on your pupil and the lesson you're giving. **Remember** - the route must be adapted to what happens in the lesson. *Don't try to pre-plan a route and stick to it - it must be adaptable!*

Your Pupil

The pupil that accompanies you on the test can be at any level of ability, but they cannot be a qualified ADI or have passed their ADI Part 2 test.

When you arrive at the test centre, it's YOUR choice whether the pupil remains in the car or accompanies you into the test centre.

Introduce your pupil to the Examiner in a relaxed way, it might be better not call them 'The Examiner', as this can make pupils nervous! Consider terms like – 'Inspector' or 'Assessor' – which aren't so scary! It might even help you to relax as well!

For most pupils, it can be slightly off-putting to have a stranger sitting in the back seat during a lesson. Explaining to your pupil that the Examiner is not interested in them or their driving, but is grading you, can help the pupil to relax.

Sometimes the Examiner (or Assessor!) might talk to the learner in order to explain that they are there to assess you and not the learner, and to check that you have reached the minimum standards required.

You must prepare for a '***normal lesson***', based on your pupil's learning needs and goals. In other words, it should be a continuation of the pupil's normal development plan.

The theme of the lesson ***could*** be one of those listed on the ADI Part 3 (SC), ***but it doesn't have to be***, it can be anything that you and your learner have agreed to work on, as long as it's the correct lesson for that pupil (more on this later in the book).

Lesson theme:	Junctions ☐	Town & city driving ☐	Interacting with other road users ☐
Dual carriageway / faster moving roads ☐	Defensive driving ☐	Effective use of mirrors ☐	
Independent driving ☐	Rural roads ☐	Motorways ☐	Eco-safe driving ☐	
Recap a manoeuvre ☐	Commentary ☐	Recap emergency stop ☐	Other ☐

The Examiner

Before the test starts the Examiner will ask you some questions about the pupil you've chosen in order to establish their level of driving skill. Questions will include:

- Roughly how many hours of lessons has your pupil had
- Whether the pupil gets any practice in between lessons from parents, friends or relatives
- Your pupils strengths and any areas for development

If you have a pupil progress record, you can show it to the Examiner if you want to. This would help explain where you are in your agreed training programme (and will also look professional!).

If you're on a trainee licence and you are charging your pupil money for the lesson, you **MUST** display your badge (when a badge is displayed, the Examiner will ask to see it). If the lesson you're giving is free, you're not required to have the badge on display.

Throughout your lesson, the examiner will be taking notes at the back of the car regarding aspects of your lesson, they are often used to form part of the de-brief at the end of the lesson.

The notes are not necessarily negative points, they could also be noting positive aspects of your lesson too. Remember that during any driving lesson you should be focusing your attention on the pupil. So, try to ignore the examiner and concentrate on your learner, and the situation around you at all times - it's what the examiner expects you to do.

Whatever the grade you receive - it's critical that you *listen carefully* to any advice the Examiner gives to you, this is because it is meant to help you enhance your skills as an ADI, and also improve future attempts at the at the Part 3 Test.

After completion of the de-brief, and after you have left the test centre, all notes from the test are destroyed.

Can anyone accompany me on the test?

You can be accompanied by your Trainer, but they are not permitted to participate in the lesson in any way, they must only be there to observe.

Other people present

Sometimes the Examiner will be accompanied by a Senior Examiner to quality assure their assessment of you. Whenever possible they will tell you in advance that this is going to happen. They will give you time to explain what's about to happen to your pupil. (the lesson can include inflating your tyres for a heavier load if you wish)

If you planned for your Trainer to accompany you, the Senior Examiner will decide whether to accompany the Examiner or not. It would mean 3 people sitting in the back of the car!!

Vehicles that can be used on the test

The vehicle used for the test must meet minimum test requirements; be roadworthy and safe.

Soft-top convertibles are *not* acceptable, nor are '2+2' vehicles where seating arrangements in the back are inadequate.

L plates (or D plates in Wales) should be fitted if you are teaching a learner - if teaching a full licence holder, they should *not* be on the vehicle.

Rear seat belts, in working order, must be fitted for the examiner to use. If there is the facility for rear head restraints these must also be fitted to ensure the Examiner's safety.

It goes without saying that suitable insurance must be in place.

If the examiner has any doubts about the suitability of your car, it could result in your test being cancelled and possibly marked as a Fail.

If you intend to use a small vehicle which has limited passenger space in the rear, you should notify the standards check booking section as soon as possible.

Rules for cars on driving tests can be found on the GOV.UK website. Here are the main points - your car must:

- be taxed

- be insured for a driving test (check with your insurance company)

- be roadworthy and have a current MOT (if it's over 3 years old)

- have no warning lights showing, for example, the airbag warning light

- have no tyre damage and the legal tread depth on each tyre

    You can't have a space-saver spare tyre fitted

- be smoke-free - this means you can't smoke in it just before or during the test

- be able to reach at least 62mph and have an mph speedometer

- have 4 wheels and a maximum authorised mass (MAM) of no more than 3,500 kg

    The MAM is the limit on how much the car can weigh when it's loaded. It will be shown in the vehicle's handbook.

On the Test

What happens at the start of the test?

When the Examiner calls your name, you will be required to confirm your identity (make sure you take your driving licence or trainee licence in with you).

The test requires you to understand all the criteria on the assessment form, the Examiner might confirm this by asking you:

> "Do you have any questions about the test before we start?"

Next, you'll be asked about your pupil, the Examiner might ask:

> "Can you tell me how many lessons your pupil has had and what you've been working on recently?"

When they're happy that they have all the information they need and that you understand what's going to happen, they will ask you to continue with your lesson, the Examiner might say:

> "Thank you………, please carry on with the lesson as you normally would."

> "I won't take any part in the lesson."

> "Please plan your lesson so that we are back at the test centre 1 hour from now"

The test will last for 1 hour (including any time at the end of the lesson for the pupil to reflect on their lesson). After this, you should allow a *minimum* of 15 minutes for a de-brief with the examiner.

The Examiner's role

The examiner's role is to assess your competence to deliver effective driving instruction. The 'National standard for driver and rider training' is expressed in terms of learning outcomes and there may be more than one way for you to achieve those outcomes.

Of course if you do, or say, something that is clearly wrong the examiner is duty bound to pick this up, especially where it could lead to a safety issue. However, the overall approach should be focused on recognising achievement and promoting improvement and development - rather than purely identifying faults.

What is the Examiner looking for?

Your job is to provide an effective learning experience for your pupil. An effective learning experience is judged to be one in which the pupil is supported to take as much responsibility as possible for their learning process.

You should, *where it is correct and safe to do so*, feel free to introduce wider issues from the driving standard into the lesson, such as assessing personal fitness to drive, the use of alcohol or drugs or dealing with aggression, however it is not a necessity.

If, for example, a pupil offers an inappropriate comment about the use of alcohol it would be appropriate for you to challenge this. Similarly, it would be appropriate for you to encourage the pupil to think through what might happen, in particular situations, if the conditions were different. For example, after negotiating a particularly difficult junction it might be helpful to discuss how different it would be at night or in bad weather.

The important thing to remember here is that the most effective learning takes place when the pupil finds the answers for themselves. If opportunities arise for discussion of issues between you and the pupil, while on the move, these can be used, but this needs to be tailored to the pupil's ability and should not create distraction.

If you can't discuss something there and then, it's worth 'flagging' it for later discussion as too many unnecessary instructions or questions from you can both de-motivate the pupil and create a real hazard.

Remember it is an offence to use a mobile phone whilst driving because this is known to create a level of risk equivalent to or, in some cases, greater than driving whilst drunk. It cannot, therefore be good practice to constantly bombard the pupil with unnecessary questions.

NOTE - If at any point during the lesson you behave in a way which puts you, the examiner, the pupil or any third party in immediate danger, the examiner will stop the lesson.

The ADI Part 3 test marking sheet:

ADI Part 3 (SC)

INFORMATION		
Candidate's name	Location	Outcome
PRN ☐☐☐☐☐	Date ☐☐ / ☐☐ / ☐☐	
I declare that my use of the test vehicle for the purposes of the test is covered by a valid policy of insurance which satisfies the requirements of the relevant legislation.	Dual Controls Yes ☐ No ☐ Reg No.	
	Log book Yes ☐ No ☐	Trainer PRN ☐☐☐☐☐☐
	Trainee Licence Yes ☐ No ☐	ORDIT Yes ☐ No ☐
	Accompanied? QA ☐ Trainer ☐ Other ☐	

ASSESSMENT

Lesson					Competence			
Student: Beginner ☐ Partly trained ☐ Trained ✓ FLH New ☐ FLH Experienced ☐					0	1	2	3
					No evidence	Demonstrated in a few elements	Demonstrated in most elements	Demonstrated in all elements

Lesson theme: Junctions ✓ Town & city driving ☐ Interacting with other road users ☐
Dual carriageway / faster moving roads ☐ Defensive driving ☐ Effective use of mirrors ☐
Independent driving ☐ Rural roads ☐ Motorways ☐ Eco-safe driving ☐
Recap a manoeuvre ☐ Commentary ☐ Recap emergency stop ☐ Other ☐

Lesson Planning	0	1	2	3
Did the trainer identify the pupil's learning goals and needs?				✓
Was the agreed lesson structure appropriate for the pupil's experience and ability?			✓	
Were the practice areas suitable?			✓	
Was the lesson plan adapted, when appropriate, to help the pupil work towards their learning goals?				✓
Score for lesson planning	10		4	6

Risk Management				
Did the trainer ensure that the pupil fully understood how the responsibility for risk would be shared?				
Were directions and instructions given to the pupil clear and given in good time?				
Was the trainer aware of the surroundings and the pupil's actions?				
Was any verbal or physical intervention by the trainer timely and appropriate?				
Was sufficient feedback given to help the pupil understand any potential safety critical incidents?				
Score for risk management				

Teaching & learning strategies				
Was the teaching style suited to the pupil's learning style and current ability?				
Was the pupil encouraged to analyse problems and take responsibility for their learning?				
Were opportunities and examples used to clarify learning outcomes?				
Was the technical information given comprehensive, appropriate and accurate?				
Was the pupil given appropriate and timely feedback during the session?				
Were the pupil's queries followed up and answered?				
Did the trainer maintain an appropriate non-discriminatory manner throughout the session?				
At the end of the session - was the pupil encouraged to reflect on their own performance?				
Score for teaching and learning strategies				
Overall score				

REVIEW	YES	NO
Did the candidate score 7 or less on Risk Management? (A 'Yes' response to this question will result in an automatic Fail)		
At any point in the lesson, did the candidate behave in a way which put you, the pupil or any third party in immediate danger, so that you had to stop the lesson? (A 'Yes' response to this question will result in an automatic Fail)		
Was advice given to seek further development?		
Feedback offered to Candidate		
Examiner Name	Signature	

How will the test be assessed?

Using the marking sheet shown opposite, the examiner will assess your lesson with 3 '*high*' areas of competence:

1. **Lesson planning**
2. **Risk Management**
3. **Teaching and Learning Strategies.**

The three '*high*' areas are broken down into a further 17 *lower* level competences. You will be given a mark for each competence. The marks will be added together to give you an overall score and provide you with a breakdown of the areas that you did well in, and areas that need further development.

The marks are broken down into 4 competence grades as follows:

0 = no evidence of competence
1 = a few elements of competence demonstrated
2 = competence demonstrated in most elements
3 = competence demonstrated in all elements

You **MUST** understand that each of the 17 lower level competences is broken down into smaller elements than those shown on the marking sheet, for example: '*Did the trainer identify the pupil's learning goals and needs?*' – is broken down further. So, to achieve a high score, the examiner will also be considering if you:

• Actively recognised the need to understand the pupil's experience and background

• Asked suitable questions

• Encouraged (not forced!!) the pupil to talk about their goals, concerns **AND LISTENED** to what the pupil had to say

• Understood the importance of what they said

• Was aware of body language or facial expressions which might have indicated that the pupil was trying to find the right words

As an example, if you look at the marking sheet on the opposite page, you can see that the candidate bought a trained pupil to the lesson in order to practice junctions.

The examiner considered the competence '*Did the trainer identify the pupil's learning goals and needs?*' then broke it down further whilst carrying out the grading.

The marks on the sheet show that the examiner thought the trainer identified the pupil's goals and needs, and adapted the lesson to help the pupil, so the trainer doesn't require further improvement in this area.

However, the examiner decided that the practice areas and the structure could have been more suited to a trained pupil, and marked each competency with a lower grade.

A literal breakdown of the competence grades by the examiner would be as follows:

3   **you don't need any further development on this area**

2   **you understand the importance of understanding your pupils needs and made a genuine effort to do, but could improve on improving your questions to draw more from your pupil**

1   **you made an attempt to understand, perhaps asked a few questions; didn't really listen and did whatever you intended regardless**

0   **you made no attempt to understand the pupil's needs**

The maximum score that you can achieve is 51. Your *overall* score will dictate your final grade:

43 – 51   **Grade A**   **A high overall standard of instruction demonstrated**

31 – 42   **Grade B**   **Sufficient competence demonstrated to permit entry to the Register of Approved Driving Instructors**

0 – 30   **Grade FAIL**   **Unsatisfactory performance**

> You **must** score a **minimum of 8** in the **Risk Management** section!

A score of 7 or less (even if your overall score is more than 31) will mean your instructional ability is substandard and will **result in a fail**.

Also, if at any point during the lesson the Examiner feels that your behaviour is putting you, the pupil or any other third party (including the Examiner) at risk, they are entitled to stop the test and record it as an **immediate fail**.

1) The partly trained, inexperienced learner

Learners at this stage are likely to want and need experience of a gradually increasing variety of road and traffic conditions to enable them to develop their basic skills.

They may have areas that they are uncomfortable with or not yet confident on, such as complex junctions or roundabouts, heavy or fast moving traffic. They may not have a good understanding of theory, or of road signs and road markings.

In this context, the key objectives of the 'National standard for driver and rider training' include you being able to:

- create a climate that promotes learning (element 6.3.1)
- explain and demonstrate skills and techniques (element 6.3.2)
- transfer the balance of responsibility for their learning process to the learner as soon as they are ready to take it (element 6.3.3)

You should be able to understand where the pupil is having difficulties and how you can help them develop good, *basic skills*.

If you are not making the effort to understand, then you are not demonstrating competence. By asking questions then listening and watching you would be making an effort to demonstrate competence.

> You don't have to achieve *full* understanding by the end of the lesson - it's '*work in progress*'

But be careful, pupils at this level should not feel that they are being patronised or talked down-to, as this will make them unreceptive. Not all pupils learn in the same way, so there is no single correct way to transfer responsibility to them - no magic formula.

Transferring responsibility is not going to happen instantly. With this in mind, you must remember that the examiner is *not expecting* you to transfer full responsibility on that lesson. The key thing is that you understand the need to transfer ownership (long term) and that you make an effort to do so in relation to the experience and ability of your learner.

You must also appreciate, at this level, that your pupil will not always 'get it right' as soon as you give them some direction or coach them around a problem.

Your goal is that the pupil understands the issue, in principle, and what they need to do in theory. You should be generally willing to help the learner overcome their weaknesses. The examiner understands that you may not be successful on that lesson, and will not penalise you if you do not immediately 'solve the issue'. You can carry on working on a particular issue during the next lesson.

You should use a variety of tools to encourage the pupil to analyse their own performance and to find solutions to problems. You should be supportive and give suitable and technically correct instructions or demonstrations where appropriate.

If your pupil cannot come up with a solution, you should provide suitable input – especially if failure to do so might result in risk to any party.

2) Experienced pupil – about to take the practical driving test

At this stage the key objective of the 'National standard for driver and rider training' is to:

- work with the learner to agree when they are ready to undertake formal assessment of driving competence (element 6.3.3)

Evidence suggests that, by this stage, some pupils may:

- be technically skilful
- be able to complete manoeuvres competently
- have experience of driving on a wide range of roads and in different types of road and traffic conditions

The pupil might be confident and feel that they are at the stage of refining their competence based on 'what they have to do to pass the test'. They could also:

- have already developed bad habits, especially if they have been taught by a friend or relative
- have an inflated opinion of their ability
- have a poor understanding of risk and danger
- have not developed the skills of scanning and planning which will help them to cope when they are driving independently
- have not developed the skills of reflection that will help them to be life-long learners (a good driver is always learning!)

They may not be used to being challenged to analyse situations and come up with solutions. They could be impatient and unresponsive to correction if they do demonstrate 'bad habits'. They may well have forgotten a lot of what they learnt when they did their theory test, or deliberately choose not to implement theory into practice.

At this level your pupil's attitude can range from enthusiastic and accepting of the information that you're giving them, to strong resistance of being told things they do not think are relevant.

During your test you must demonstrate that you understand the key issues that need to be addressed to try to reduce the numbers of newly qualified drivers who crash in the first 6 months of passing their test.

You should be working with your pupil to develop a realistic understanding of ability and an enhanced understanding of risk.

You should be checking, developing and reinforcing systematic scanning and planning tools and strongly encouraging pupils to reflect on their own driving.

You should be supportive, but not over-instruct, you must give suitable and technically correct instructions and / or demonstrations where necessary.

However, the emphasis is likely to be on the use of tools such as practical examples, to develop a more 'joined-up' and outward looking approach - help your learner to see the 'bigger picture' so they aren't just focusing on 'passing the test'.

3) New full licence holder (FLH)

Although the New FLH has demonstrated that they are safe to drive by passing their driving test. Both the theory and practical test are limited in what the candidate is actually tested on. For example, they don't require the pupil to drive on all classes of roads and they don't test understanding of the part of the NDS (National Driver Standards) which calls on learners to reflect on their competence as they go through their driving career.

Your objective as an instructor should be to develop the pupil's competence and ability across the *full range of driving scenarios* and to support and encourage a commitment to life-long learning around driving.

Reasons why a FLH might come to you for further training at this stage could include:

- wanting to refresh their skills if they haven't driven since they took their test
- moving on to a bigger or technologically different vehicle
- starting to drive for work
- starting a family and wanting to improve their skills
- moving from an urban to rural environment, or vice versa
- starting to use motorways
- a simple desire to become a better developed driver

If the pupil has *chosen to take training*, they are likely to be keen and enthusiastic and, in theory, open to learning.

If, on the other hand, they have been told to take it, perhaps by an employer, they might be resentful and resistant.

They may well have lost the disciplines of the mirrors-signal-manoeuvre (MSM) routine and forward planning. They may not be used to driving in an 'Eco-Safe' way and may not even understand the term. They may be nervous about increased responsibility and accountability.

During your test, the key thing that you must demonstrate is that you are able to find out exactly what the pupil wants from that lesson, and formulate a plan to deliver that. You must of course, identify and deal with any bad habits that might have been acquired.

However, if all you do is cover what the pupil should have learnt prior to their test, you are unlikely to reinforce commitment to life-long learning.

4) Experienced full licence holder (FLH)

At this stage the Experienced FLH pupil should be more confident and competent than they were immediately on passing their test. They could have many years of experience and should have gained exposure on all or most of the possible classes of roads, at night and in bad weather.

They may already be driving for work and are likely to think of themselves as capable drivers, even though their application of safety routines and forward planning skills may show that they are not quite as competent as they think they are!

Reasons why an individual may come to an Instructor at this stage of driving include:

- being required by employers to undertake additional training to keep insurance costs down
- wanting to drive more economically to reduce business costs
- having had an accident or a near miss that has shaken their confidence
- returning to driving after a period of ill-health or loss of licence
- recognising that their driving skills are deteriorating through age or ill health

The FLH maybe an overseas driver who has sufficient experience but is now required to take the tests to qualify for a UK licence.

Depending on *their reasons* for undertaking training these pupils could be enthusiastic or very nervous; willing or very resistant.

Older pupils may find it harder to learn new skills or to get out of bad habits. They may have developed unsafe habits such as not leaving large enough separation distances and failing to carry out systematic observation routines.

During the session the key thing is that you must demonstrate that you can find out exactly what the pupil wants from that lesson, and put together a plan to deliver that. You must, of course, spot and deal with bad habits that might have been acquired.

However, the lesson must take the pupil *forward in their learning*; the Examiner does not want to see you making an experienced FLH drive like a good learner. If the lesson does not deliver what the pupil is looking for they will not engage or connect with the learning process.

Please note: This is NOT an exhaustive and comprehensive list of possible scenarios; they are simply outlines of the typical type of lesson for the ability and level of the pupil that you take. It's purpose is to give you an idea of the sort of things that should be considered.

The Competence Framework explained...

The purpose of all driver-training is to assess and develop the learner's skill, knowledge and understanding in relation to the NSDRT (National Standard for Driver and Rider Training, you'll find this at the back of this book).

Research shows that that this best achieved by placing the client / learner at the **centre of the learning process**.

In the following section of the book we have explained each of the 17 'lower level' sub competences and highlighted what you should be doing plus explained the mistakes that you **MUST** avoid. We've highlighted key points within each competence to help you understand how to conduct a '**client centred**' approach to your lessons.

Section 1: Lesson Planning

Lesson Planning					
Did the trainer identify the pupil's learning goals and needs?					
Was the agreed lesson structure appropriate for the pupil's experience and ability?					
Were the practice areas suitable?					
Was the lesson plan adapted, when appropriate, to help the pupil work towards their learning goals?					
Score for lesson planning					

'Client **centred**' learning does not mean 'client **led**', the learner is not making all the decisions on what they learn or how they learn it, instead, it's about working **in partnership** with your learner.

Traditionally, driving lessons have been conducted in an 'instructor led' manner; some learners are very happy for the ADI to make the decisions. In this style of teaching the instructor, with experience and expertise decides on what will happen next.

Lesson planning **WITH** your learner has proven to encourage **long-term positive attitudes to driving safely.** Learners that are told what to do and taught how to pass a test will quickly forget what they have been taught.

1. Did the trainer identify the pupil's learning goals & needs?

Usually this aspect will take place at the beginning of the lesson. However when you and the pupil have been **working together** for some time, you may have already discussed the basic structure of the pupil's learning goals.

It is also important to remember that a better understanding of the pupils needs may change as the lesson progresses. Therefore, you need to remain alert as this aspect is not just something that can be mentioned at the start of the lesson and then forgotten about, it can change as the lesson progresses.

A PDI that demonstrates a *high level for this competence* could be:

- encouraging pupils to say what *they would want* from the lesson
- asking questions to ensure understanding of the topics
- checking understanding of the lesson progresses
- listening to what the pupil is saying
- and paying close attention to body language

A PDI that demonstrates a *lack of competence* in this aspect could be:

- making assumptions about understanding or experience
- failing to note negative or concerned comments
- failing to note body language that shows discomfort or confusion
- undermining the pupils confidence by continuously asking questions which are clearly too difficult for the learner to answer
- forcing the pupil to address issues that they are not happy to talk about unless there is a need, such as an identified risk safety critical issue

2. Was the agreed lesson structure appropriate for the pupil's experience and ability?

The lesson structure should allow the pupil to progress *at a manageable rate*; stretching them without overwhelming them.

For example the pupil who is concerned about entering roundabouts should not be asked to tackle a fast flowing multilane multi-junction as their first attempt!

Neither should they be restricted to very quiet junctions, unless you have identified potential safety issues that you would like to check out first. This aspect is about pitching the lesson correctly on that day.

A PDI that demonstrates a *high level for this competence* in all elements of the lesson should be:

- ensuring the pupil understands what they plan to do and agrees with that plan
- conducting lesson that reflects the information given by the pupil and the learning goals *they wanted* to work on
- building opportunities to check the progress made by people before moving on to more challenging situations
- checking theoretical understanding

Common mistakes which show a *lack of competence* in this aspect could be:

- delivering a pre-planned, standard lesson that does not take into account the pupils expressed needs or concerns
- failing to build in a suitable balance of practice and theory

3. Were the practice areas suitable?

The area that you use and the route you take during the lesson, should allow the pupil to practice safely and help them to achieve their goals. It should stretch your pupil but not be overly challenging. You should not take your pupil out of their competence zone.

A PDI that demonstrates a *high level for this competence* in all elements of the lesson should be choosing a practice area / route that provide:

- a range of opportunities to address the *agreed learning objectives*
- challenges the pupil, but is realistic in terms of the pupil's capabilities and confidence

Common mistakes which show a *lack of competence* in this aspect could be:

- taking the pupil outside of their competence so that they spend all their time 'surviving' and have no space or time left to look at what the learning issues are
- exposing the pupil to risks that they cannot manage

4. Was the lesson adapted, where appropriate to help the pupil work towards their learning goals?

As an Instructor you should be ready and willing to adapt the lesson if the pupil:

- appears to be uncomfortable or unable to deal with the lesson that you have setup or the topics that you had agreed to work on
- if the pupil suggests that the lesson is not providing what they set out to achieve

If the pupil is creating risk due to inability you must adapt the lesson quickly!

Your lesson *must reflect and change to the learner 'on that day'*. Many learners will not be themselves when an Examiner is in the back of the car, be prepared to adapt or change the plan completely if necessary.

Whatever the reason may be for adapting the plan, you must make sure the pupil understands what you are doing and why you're doing it.

A PDI that demonstrates a *high level for this competence* in all elements of the lesson should be:

- comparing the actual performance of the pupil with their ability and verifying any differences
- responding to any faults or weaknesses that undermine the original plan of the lesson
- reacting to any questions or concerns raised by the pupil
- picking up on body language which may show discomfort or confusion

Common mistakes which show a *lack of competence* in this aspect could be:

- continuing with the planned lesson despite the pupil being clearly out of their depth
- continuing with the planned lesson despite the pupil demonstrating faults or weaknesses in ability which require a rethink of the plan
- changing the plan without reason
- not explaining to the learner why the plan has been changed

Section 2: Risk Management

Risk Management					
Did the trainer ensure that the pupil fully understood how the responsibility for risk would be shared?					
Were directions and instructions given to the pupil clear and given in good time?					
Was the trainer aware of the surroundings and the pupil's actions?					
Was any verbal or physical intervention by the trainer timely and appropriate?					
Was sufficient feedback given to help the pupil understand any potential safety critical incidents?					
Score for risk management					

It is vital that all parties in any on-road training situation understand, and are clear about, where the responsibility lies for the safety of themselves, others in the vehicle and to other road users.

There are two aspects to the management of risk in any training situation.

At all times, **you the PDI are responsible for your safety, the safety of the pupil and the safety of other road users**. In some cases this could lead to taking physical control of the vehicle to manage safety critical incidents. If you fail in this basic responsibility at any time, **you will fail your Part 3 test!**

From the training point of view, you are also responsible for developing the pupil's awareness of, and ability to manage risk (as the driver, the pupil also has some responsibility). This is the objective that is being assessed in this section.

5. Did the trainer ensure the pupil fully understood how the responsibility for risk would be shared?

The 'balance of responsibility' between the pupil and you will vary in different circumstances. For example:

> **a)** A pupil in the very early stages of their training, in a car fitted with dual controls.

In this situation you could start a lesson by saying something like:

> *"I expect you to drive carefully and responsibly as possible at all times. I will expect you to be aware of other road users and to control the car. I do have the ability to take control of the car in an emergency if I need to. I would only use these controls when I feel that you are not dealing with the situation yourself. If that happens we can take some time to discuss it so that you understand for next time"*

In different circumstances:

> **b)** a pupil who has passed their driving test but has asked you to give them some additional training in their own car, the car is much bigger and more technically advanced than the one they learnt in.

In this situation you might say something like:

> *"As you have passed your test I would assume that you are taking full responsibility for our safety. I will be talking to you from time to time but I will try to keep that to a minimum so that I don't distract you. If I'm quiet it means that I am comfortable with what you are doing so don't worry. I will of course let you know if I see any risk or hazard that you appear to have missed"*

(examples 'a' and 'b' are for illustration purposes only)

These opening statements are not all that is involved in meeting this competence. You should be managing this process continuously throughout your lesson. If for example the pupil makes some sort of mistake while carrying out a manoeuvre, you should discuss and analyse the mistake with the pupil.

Having achieved an understanding of what went wrong you might ask the pupil to try the manoeuvre again. At this point you should provide the pupil with clear information regarding what is required of them.

For example, if the pupil is trained you could say something like:

> *"Let's try that manoeuvre again. I won't say anything but remember what we had just been talking about"*

If the pupil is in the early stages of driving, you could say something like:

> *"Let's try that again, I'll guide you through it. Follow my instructions"*

You need to work with your pupil to decide the best way of dealing with the problem; this may mean a temporary change regarding the responsibility of the safety. The important thing is that the pupil is made aware of what is expected of them.

Under test conditions there are no circumstances in which you can assume that the issue of risk management has been dealt with. Even if you and a pupil had discussions about risk on previous lessons, **you must show that you are actively managing this issue for assessment purposes**.

A PDI that demonstrates a **high level for this competence** in all elements of the lesson could be:

- asking the pupil what is meant by risk
- asking the pupil what type of issues can create risk
- explaining clearly what is expected of the pupil and what the pupil can expect of you during the lesson
- checking that the pupil understands what is required from them when there is a change of plan or if they are asked to repeat an exercise

Common mistakes which show a lack of competence in this aspect include:

- failing to address the issue of risk management
- giving incorrect guidance regarding responsibility for the management of risk
- failing to explain how or when dual controls might be used
- not encouraging a pupil's commitment to being safe and responsible
- not explaining your role when repeating an exercise or manoeuvre

6. Were directions and instructions given to the pupil clear and given in good time?

'Directions' should be taken to mean any instruction, such as 'take the next road on the left' or 'make sure the clutch comes up earlier'. **Any input** from you must be sufficient, timely and appropriate.

It is important that you are **taking account of the ability of your learner** when giving directions. Late, misleading or confusing directions or instructions do not allow the pupil to respond correctly and can make things worse if for example your pupil suddenly comes to a stop on a main road.

Too many unnecessary instructions from you can de-motivate your learner and create a real hazard. It is not good practice to be constantly bombarding your learner with unnecessary questions; it can be severely distracting and can create a high level of risk.

A PDI that demonstrates a **high level for this competence** in all elements of the lesson should:

- be giving directions at a suitable time so that the pupil can respond
- be giving clear, concise directions and instructions

Common mistakes which show a **lack of competence** in this aspect include:

- giving confused directions
- giving the pupil late directions
- giving unnecessary directions or instructions
- not recognising that your input is confusing or overloading the learner

7. Was the trainer aware of the surroundings and the pupil's actions?

This competence lies at the core of your professional skill. You should be able to:

- be aware of the situation around you at all times
- be aware of the actions of your pupil, including body language and any comments
- judge whether your pupil's actions are suitable in relation to any situation
- respond quickly and accordingly

8. Was any verbal or physical intervention by the trainer timely and appropriate?

The overall balance regarding this competence should be *pupil-centred*. There is a fine balance between too much input and not giving enough input.

Any input from you should *be appropriate to the pupil and the situation*. If you're stationary it could take the form of a discussion with your pupil. If you're on the move and your pupil is doing well, keeping quiet and signalling your confidence in your pupil (through your body language) is just as productive as asking them correctly timed questions.

The most important 'interventions' are those that are managing risk when the vehicle is moving. You would be expected to be proactive in pointing out situations where a risk or hazard may arise.

Sometimes direct intervention by you, to prevent a situation getting worse, may be needed. This competence is about your response to these situations.

A PDI that demonstrates a *high level for this competence* in all elements of the lesson should be:

- taking control of the situation when the pupil is clearly out of their depth
- intervening in a way that supports the pupils learning process and safety during the lesson
- knowing when to allow the pupil to deal with situations appropriately

Common mistakes which show a *lack of competence* in this aspect include:

- ignoring a developing hazard and leaving the pupil to struggle
- taking control of the situation when it is not necessary
- intervening when it is not necessary
- intervening inappropriately and distracting your learner
- undermining the people's confidence
- making yourself the person who is in sole control of the lesson

9. Was sufficient feedback given to help the pupil understand any potentially safety critical incidents?

If a safety critical or potentially critical incident does occur, *it is vital that the pupil fully understands what happened and how they could have avoided or dealt with it better*.

Ideally the pupil should be supported to analyse the situation for themselves. However it is not always necessary for you to provide feedback immediately, especially if your learner did not see the problem. In that case the feedback should be given as soon as is practicable after the incident.

A PDI that demonstrates a *high level for this competence* in all elements of the lesson could be:

- finding a safe place to stop and discuss the incident
- allowing the pupil time to discuss any concerns the incident may have caused
- helping the pupil to reflect on what happened
- clarifying aspects of the incident that the pupil may not have understood
- providing guidance when the pupil does not understand what they should do differently
- checking that the pupil feels able to put the strategy in place
- discussing ways to help the learner deal with the same situation if they need it

Common mistakes which show a *lack of competence* in this aspect include:

- forgetting to discuss the incident
- taking too long to address any issues regarding the incident
- not allowing the pupil to discuss their own understanding of the incident
- telling the pupil what the solution is but not checking the pupils understanding
- failing to check the pupil's ability to be able to respond to a similar situation when it arises

Section 3: Teaching and Learning Strategies

Teaching & learning strategies					
Was the teaching style suited to the pupil's learning style and current ability?					
Was the pupil encouraged to analyse problems and take responsinility for their learning?					
Were opportunities and examples used to clarify learning outcomes?					
Was the technical information given comprehensive, appropriate and accurate?					
Was the pupil given appropriate and timely feedback during the session?					
Were the pupil's queries followed up and answered?					
Did the trainer maintain an appropriate non-discriminatory manner throughout the session?					
At the end of the session - was the pupil encouraged to reflect on their own performance?					
Score for teaching and learning strategies					

The important thing to remember when considering teaching and learning styles is that it is **not just about coaching**. It is about **pupil-centred** learning. You need to make sure that you can help your pupil to learn in an active way. Instruction based around the core competencies must not be forgotten. As an Instructor your objective is to increase your options.

Coaching is just another option; it is not an automatic replacement for any other existing method.

There are many occasions when it is useful to use coaching techniques. The principle behind coaching is that an engaged pupil is likely to achieve a higher level of understanding, plus solutions which are worked out by his or herself are far more relevant to the learner, rather than simply being told how to do it.

Direct instruction or guidance is useful and necessary in helping the pupil in the early stages when dealing with new situations or when helping the pupil who is struggling.

Good coaching is about using the correct technique at the correct time. If you need to give direct instruction through a particularly difficult situation, the instruction given is part of the coaching process providing you then encourage your learner to analyse what happened and discuss how they can learn from it.

10. Was the teaching style suited to the pupil's learning style and current ability?

You need to take into account all that you understand about your pupil. You should be aware that **different pupils learn in different ways**. Your pupil's 'learning style' may only become apparent after many lessons, and can vary from lesson to lesson and topic.

You should be able to show evidence regarding some sensitivity to these issues. In a one-hour lesson the best way to demonstrate this is to offer a range of options. You should have the flexibility to adjust your teaching style to match the learner's learning style.

It is impossible to make somebody learn. A pupil's progress will depend on what the pupil is comfortable with on that day. Your skill is to recognise when a learner has had enough and has stopped learning but also to pace your lesson in relation to your learner - making the lesson challenging enough but not too challenging.

You should ensure that the teaching tools you are using are suitable. If a question and answer technique is used, it must match the pupil's level of ability to ensure they are able to answer the questions and encourage a higher level of thinking. Asking open questions to a novice learner can be very confusing and deflating. *You will be assessed on the effectiveness of your teaching style based on the circumstances at that time*.

A PDI that demonstrates a *high level for this competence* in all elements of the lesson could be:

- actively working to understand how they can best support the pupil's learning (the learner might not achieve a full understanding on this lesson - it is the attempt that you make which is being assessed)
- changing your teaching style when necessary
- giving accurate and technically correct instruction and information (giving technically incorrect information or instruction is an automatic fail if the input might lead to a safety critical incident)
- using practical examples or other tools to provide a different perspective on the topic
- linking theory to practical
- encouraging the learner to take more ownership of their learning process
- responding to faults quickly and correctly
- providing enough uninterrupted time that the learner to practice something new
- providing the pupil which strategies on how they might practice or learn in their own time outside of the lesson

Common mistakes which show a *lack of competence* in this aspect include:

- using the incorrect teaching style in relation to the pupils learning style
- not agreeing with the learner to make sure your teaching style is acceptable
- not attempting to try other ways of addressing a particular teaching or learning point
- concentrating on teaching and learning styles but ignoring the learning outcomes
- ignoring safety

11. Was the pupil encouraged to analyse problems and take responsibility for their learning?

A key part of the pupil-centred teaching approach is to develop active problem-solving in the learner. This means that you have to *provide time for this to happen and you have to stop talking long enough to allow the pupil to do the work*.

The key thing to remember is that different pupils will respond in different ways. Some learners may respond immediately in a discussion, other learners may need to reflect on a particular problem when they are away from the lesson. You may need to encourage them to read or research to help them understand a particular issue or problem. Pushing a pupil for an answer on the spot may be unproductive and demoralising to some pupils. The key word here is '*encouraged*' not forced!

A PDI that demonstrates a *high level for this competence* in all elements of the lesson could be:

- choosing suitable places to allow time to discuss any problems or issues that arose during the lesson
- providing opportunities for analysis; quickly in the case of high risk incidences
- using and taking time to understand any problems the pupil is having with understanding
- offering strategies to help the pupil develop, this could be practical or theoretical
- giving clear and accurate advice to fill any gaps in the pupils knowledge or understanding
- giving the pupil a sense of responsibility for their learning

Common mistakes which show a *lack of competence* in this aspect include:

- leaving the pupil with a sense that the instructor was in full control of the teaching process
- not showing flexibility in using different ways of dealing with a problem - especially in relation to a learner's desire for a different teaching style
- giving unsuitable or incorrect input during the lesson

12. Were opportunities and examples used to clarify learning outcomes?

While it's important to train a learner in technique, it's vital to link the technique with the theory behind it. *The best way to do this is to use live examples during the session*.

The use of live examples and scenarios will give the learner a deeper understanding of why the use of a particular method or technique was important at that time.

An example of this could be done by asking the pupil why they think it's important to look through the rear window when reversing.

A PDI that demonstrates a *high level for this competence* in all elements of the lesson could be:

- using examples identified on the lesson in a suitable way and at a suitable time
- using different ways of giving examples in relation to a learner's preferred learning style
- giving examples that the pupil can understand in relation to their current ability and life experience
- being aware that some pupils can respond immediately and other pupils may need to think about the issue

Common mistakes which show a *lack of competence* in this aspect include:

- using examples that your pupil cannot understand due to a lack of experience
- using examples that are far too complicated for the pupil to respond to
- not allowing time for the pupil think through a particular issue
- not allowing the pupil an opportunity to voice their opinion

13. Was the technical information given comprehensive, appropriate and accurate?

As mentioned earlier giving incorrect or insufficient information may result in an automatic fail if the result of that information can lead to a critical or high risk situation.

Good information is:

- accurate
- relevant
- timely

If one of the above criteria is not met, then the other criteria become redundant!

Most driving lessons will require some technical advice from the Instructor, this could be to solve a problem or fill a gap in the pupil's knowledge. The advice given **MUST** be accurate and appropriate.

If giving a practical demonstration, it must be clear and suitable for the learner. The pupil should be involved and given a chance to understand what they are being shown.

Advice that is given unnecessarily may not be of any use, for example if you are continuously guiding the pupil on what to do and how to do it you are not allowing the pupil to take any responsibility or understanding of what they are trying to achieve. If the advice you gave is unclear or misleading it can confuse your learner.

A PDI that demonstrates a *high level for this competence* in all elements of the lesson could be:

- giving clear, accurate and well timed explanations or demonstrations
- insuring the pupil understands and, if necessary repeating the demonstration or explanation
- exploring different methods to demonstrate or explain if the pupil still does not understand

Common mistakes which show a *lack of competence* in this aspect include:

- giving unclear or inaccurate information
- providing information too late or too early during the lesson
- not checking the pupil's understanding
- not exploring different ways of explaining the situation when the pupil doesn't understand the first time

14. Was the pupil given appropriate and timely feedback during the session?

Feedback is a vital part of any learning process but it must be given in a balanced way. *Your pupil needs a clear picture of how they are doing in relation to their learning goals*.

Positive feedback should be given quickly when the learner is performing well. Negative feedback needs to be given at a suitable time and in a suitable place. Bombarding your learner with information about the fault (at an unsuitable time), can be de-motivating and dangerous.

Sometimes just sitting quietly and saying nothing can also be a form of feedback - *it depends on the situation and the experience and ability of your pupil*.

The feedback you gave should be truthful, positive and correct. It is not helping your learner to give unrealistic feedback; it will give them a false sense of their ability. However, giving negative feedback should be done in a positive way, using it as a learning point. But if the learner needs to be told that they are doing something wrong or dangerous you must be direct and to the point. *The pupil needs a true sense and realisation of their performance*.

It is important to listen to your pupil's questions or comments; your pupil's feedback should never be overlooked or ignored.

A PDI that demonstrates a *high level for this competence* in all elements of the lesson could be:

- giving prompt feedback when asked questions by the pupil
- using opportunities in giving feedback which reinforces the learner's understanding or achievement of their learning goals
- giving feedback regarding the failure to reach their learning goals which then helps the pupil to understand what they need to improve on
- giving feedback in a way that the pupil understands you
- being consistent with feedback and use of positive body language

Common mistakes which show a *lack of competence* in this aspect include:

- giving feedback too long after an incident or situation has occurred so that the pupil cannot remember what happened
- giving feedback that ignores a safety critical incident
- giving continuous feedback when it's distracting the pupil
- not checking the pupil's understanding of the feedback given
- ignoring or failing to listen to feedback about your own performance

15. Were the pupil's queries followed up and answered?

Any questions or queries from the pupil must be dealt with as soon as possible. Your answer could be providing information to the learner or directing your learner to a suitable reference such as books or the Internet.

If possible, the pupil should be encouraged to discover answers for themselves - this way they will develop a better understanding of a topic rather than just knowing the answer. If you need to give your learner the answer you must ensure they fully understand the information that you gave them.

Some pupils don't have the confidence to ask direct questions, you should be able to pick up on their body language or comments which may indicate a lack of understanding or confusion.

A PDI that demonstrates a *high level for this competence* in all elements of the lesson could be:

- responding honestly and quickly to questions
- giving helpful answers and/or directing the pupil to reference material
- responding to body language or comments from the pupil and checking if they have any doubts or uncertainties
- encouraging the learner to consider answers to their questions themselves (in relation to ability and experience)

Common mistakes which show a *lack of competence* in this aspect include:

- not responding to questions
- giving incorrect advice in relation to questions asked
- avoiding the question or denying responsibility for answering a question

16. Did the trainer maintain an appropriate, non-discriminatory manner throughout the session?

During your lesson you must create an atmosphere in which your learner is comfortable to express opinion and ask questions. *You should have an open, friendly and relaxed environment for teaching regardless* of the pupil's age, religion, gender, ethnic background, sexual orientation, physical ability or any other factor. This includes respect for your pupil's values and culture.

You must not display any inappropriate or judgemental behaviour or attitude towards other road users and should also challenge your pupil if they display such behaviour.

A PDI that demonstrates a *high level for this competence* in all elements of the lesson should be:

- not entering the pupils personal space and keeping a respectable distance from them
- sitting in an appropriate position in the car
- not using derogatory or discriminatory language towards other road users
- challenging the pupil regarding any discriminatory attitudes

Common mistakes which show a *lack of competence* in this aspect include:

- invading a learner's personal space
- touching the pupil
- trying to shake hands with the pupil (this can be frowned upon depending on culture and background)
- using somebody's first name or shortening their name unless the pupil has agreed that this is acceptable
- commenting on your learner's dress code or appearnce unless it has a direct relationship on their ability to drive, i.e. wearing shoes that make it difficult to operate the pedals

17. At the end of the session was the pupil encouraged to reflect on their own performance?

At the end of the lesson the pupil should be encouraged to reflect on their performance and discuss how they feel their lesson went. You should encourage honest self-appraisal and use 'pupil centred' techniques to highlight areas that you and the learner feel need to be developed.

Topics and subjects discussed here should be agreed for development on future lessons.

Again, the key word here is '*encouraged*', not all pupils are able to reflect on the spot. You should know your pupil and encourage them to reflect on their lesson in their own way and in their own time if necessary. You could ask your learner to think about how they feel the lesson went and compare ideas on the next lesson.

What happens at the end of the test?

Once you've finished any discussions with your pupil and the lesson has come to an end, the Examiner will tell you that the test has finished, they might say:

"Thank you ………….., I'll now go and complete my paperwork. This will take about 10-15 minutes. I will then come and find you to give you some feedback on the lesson. You're both welcome to wait here or to sit in the waiting room"

The Examiner *will not* de-brief you with your pupil present, you can have your Trainer present for the de-brief but they cannot take part in the discussion.

Feedback from the Examiner

When the examiner has finished filling in the assessment form they will inform you of the grade you have achieved and whther you have passed or failed. If you have been assessed as a Fail you will be told clearly that your instruction is not at an acceptable level.

The examiner will then give you more detailed feedback relating to the competences against which you have been assessed:

- lesson planning
- risk management
- teaching and learning strategies

The purpose of feedback is to help you to understand where you failed to demonstrate full competence and where you need to focus your efforts when undertaking further training and development. You should not feel that you have done something wrong. You must understand what has led to the grade that has been awarded.

The assessment form will be able to show you the 'profile' of your performance against the individual competences, very clearly. This should help you to see where you have given a strong performance as well as where you need development.

The examiner will not produce any additional written reports or follow-up letters.

However, it is important to remember that the examiner *will NOT tell you what you should have done*, that is for you to reflect on and to think on how to improve your own performance.

Alternatively, seek advice from a reputable ORDIT registered trainer.

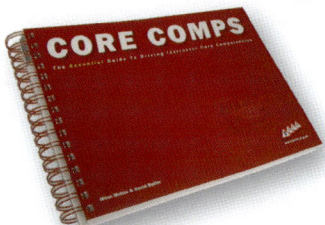

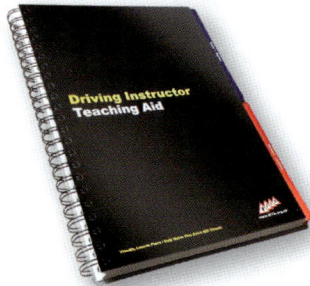

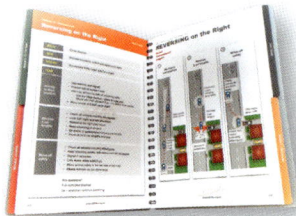

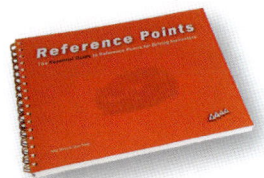

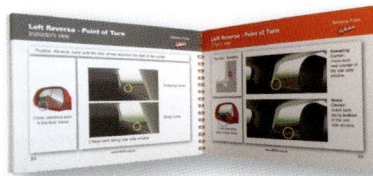

**The following pages are taken from the
Driving & Vehicle Standards Agency document:**

National Standard for driver and rider training (NSDRT)

PDF File can be found at www.gov.uk

PDF file: https://www.gov.uk/government/uploads/system/uploads/attachment_data/file/
377667/national-standard-for-driver-and-rider-training.pdf

PDF file reference: DVSA/NS/DRT

Contents

Introducing the 'National standard for driver and rider training'

This national standard sets out the skills, knowledge and understanding needed to deliver a programme of driver/rider training. It covers training for drivers or riders of all types of cars, light vans, motorcycles and mopeds for use on the road. It covers training for licence acquisition and post-test driving/riding programmes.

The standard assumes that any person wishing to teach somebody to drive or ride has

- a current driving/riding licence

- mastered all the competences set out in roles 1 to 4 of the 'National standard for driving cars and light vans (category B)' or the 'National standard for riding mopeds and motorcycles (category A)'

- demonstrated competence in role 5 of the 'National standard for driving cars and light vans (category B)' or the 'National standard for riding mopeds and motorcycles (category A)'

In other words it assumes that they have maintained and improved their competence, at both the theoretical and practical levels, since they acquired their licence. Candidates will be expected to demonstrate at least level 3 competence.

This standard sets out the knowledge, skills and understanding needed to deliver successful learning. It talks about instructors delivering agreed syllabuses using a 'client-centred' approach. The Standard talks mainly about the skills, knowledge and understanding required to work 'in-car' (or 'on bike') but also acknowledges that some driver/rider training organisations may opt to deliver part of any given syllabus to a classroom group. The knowledge, skills and understanding that apply in the classroom have therefore been included, but not all instructors will choose to train in this way. For motorcycle instructors, however, group delivery in a classroom (or similar training environment) is a core skill.

The standard includes some of the skills, knowledge and understanding needed by trainers of instructors (such as role play). It assumes higher level assessment skills will be covered by a standard assessor unit.

As with all of the Driver and Vehicle Standards Agency's (DVSA's) standards, this standard is expected to change in response to further evidence that may emerge and to peer comment. It is expected that the range of units will be extended to cover specialist areas such as the Equality Act and the delivery of remedial programmes.

Note:

These units were used as the basis for redefining the Driver Training National Occupational Standards, which are used to develop any driver training qualifications.

Role 6 – Deliver driver/rider training programmes

Unit 1 – Prepare to train learner driver/riders – meet all legal requirements

What this unit is about

This unit is about confirming that you meet all the legal requirements before you start delivering training. These cover

- the vehicle or machine you intend to use

- your status as an instructor

The core of this unit is that you must know and understand what the law says about using a vehicle or machine for training purposes and about your entitlement to deliver training.

Some of the tasks may be given to other people in your organisation. However, you should still be able to confirm that the vehicle you intend to use is roadworthy and that you are legally able to carry out the training.

This unit contains two elements

Element 6.1.1 – Confirm that you comply with legal requirements

Element 6.1.2 – Confirm that the training vehicle is fit for purpose

Who this unit is for

This unit is for instructors who train learner driver/riders.

Glossary

Your organisation:	*This is the company you work for or, if you are self employed, the rules you have set for yourself to make sure you comply with relevant legal and licensing requirements.*
Vehicle:	*This covers all powered means of travel, such as cars, motorcycles, vans, etc.*
Driver/rider:	*This includes drivers or riders of all vehicles.*
Learner:	*This term can indicate novice, partly trained, trained or experienced driver/riders, including those who may be adding a licence category.*

National standard for driver and rider training   www.gov.uk/dvsa/driving-standards

Unit 6.1 – Prepare to train learner driver/riders – meet all legal requirements

Element 6.1.1 – Confirm that you comply with legal requirements

About this element

This element is about making sure that you can legally provide training. This includes licence and instructor registration requirements. You must report any change to your health or eyesight, or any convictions, to all those who legally need to know.

Performance standards	Knowledge and understanding requirements
You must be able to	You must know and understand
1. confirm that you hold a current, valid licence to drive or ride the training vehicle	a. the licence regulations that apply to the training vehicle you are using
2. confirm that you are registered as an instructor with the appropriate body or bodies, or that you are exempt from registration	b. whether there are requirements to belong to a register of instructors for the training vehicle you are using
3. comply with organisational and legal requirements to report any change to your status as an instructor, such as	c. the legal requirements and conditions that apply to gaining and maintaining registration to any appropriate body or bodies
• convictions	d. the types of offence you must report under organisational or legal requirements and how they affect your status as an instructor
• medical conditions	
• changes to your eyesight	e. how changes to your health or your eyesight may affect your status as an instructor
4. display your current instructor registration certificate, or have it with you, in line with legal requirements	f. the eyesight requirements that apply for the training vehicle you are using

Unit 6.1 – Prepare to train learner driver/riders – meet all legal requirements

Element 6.1.2 - Confirm that the training vehicle is fit for purpose

---

About this element

This element is about making sure the training vehicle meets the relevant legal and organisational requirements for roadworthiness. Where the vehicle is a motorcycle or moped, it should also be suitable for the rider. You should confirm that all necessary documentation is available and valid. You should also be aware of any requirements for a minimum test vehicle (MTV). Routine maintenance and recognising any faults with the vehicle are also covered.

When using a vehicle provided by the learner there are clearly limits to how far you can go in carrying out checks and taking corrective actions. You should still confirm that the vehicle meets MTV requirements, check the documentation, carry out basic safety checks, such as those on tyres and lights, and make sure that L plates (or D plates in Wales) are displayed correctly.

Performance standards	Knowledge and understanding requirements
You must be able to	You must know and understand

1. make sure that any vehicle used for training purposes
 	
  • meets the minimum test vehicle requirements
 	
  • is correctly marked
	a. minimum test vehicle (MTV) requirements for licence acquisition practical tests
	
	b. the legal requirement to identify a vehicle being used for on-road training of provisional licence holders, by fitting L/D plates

2. make sure that any ancillary equipment fitted to the vehicle, such as dual controls, satellite navigation systems* or other electronic aids, is
 	
  • legally compliant
 	
  • fit for purpose
	c. how to check the operation of equipment such as dual controls
	
	d. any legal requirements or restrictions that apply to the fitting and use of ancillary equipment and how to make sure it can be used safely and with the minimum of distraction

3. make sure that insurance is in place to cover driver/rider-training, and where appropriate driver/rider-testing, in the vehicle as adapted	e. what insurance you must have in place to deliver driver/rider documentation (such as registration, tax disc and MOT) meets legal requirements
4. confirm all other vehicle	

*DVSA is aware that satellite navigation systems can take a variety of forms; embedded within the manufacturer's standard equipment, free-standing/post-market or smartphone app. The technology is also evolving rapidly. The use of the phrase 'satellite navigation system' in this standard is taken to mean any electronic device, of whatever format, that is used as an aid to navigation.

5. confirm the vehicle's service record is in accordance with the supplier's or your organisation's recommendations

6. carry out vehicle checks and report faults or problems with the vehicle in line with organisational and legal requirements

7. carry out corrective actions that are within your authority

8. make other arrangements when a vehicle is not fit for purpose

f. the need to inform your insurance provider of any adaptations to your vehicle

g. the statutory registration, licensing and testing requirements for the vehicle

h. how to access the service record for the vehicle and confirm that necessary servicing has been carried out

i. how to access any organisational checklist for the vehicle and carry out those checks

j. what action to take if the vehicle

- does not have all the necessary documentation

- has not been serviced

- fails any checks

Role 6 - Deliver driver/rider training programmes

Role 6 Unit 2 – Design learning programmes

What this unit is about

This unit uses a 'client-centred' learning approach. It is about maximising learning by taking into account the status, prior experience and particular needs of the learner.

This unit assumes that any instructor should be able to respond to the needs of any individual who wishes to be trained. It is unreasonable to expect an instructor to understand, and be able to respond to, the specific needs of every type of special need. However, they should be able to actively manage the process of finding alternative support in these circumstances.

Instructors may be following outline programmes designed by others. As a learner-centred instructor, however, they must be able to adjust an outline programme to meet the needs of the learner by

- taking prior learning into account

- identifying any issues or opportunities as the training progresses

They must also understand how adjustments will affect the learning outcomes of the programme. They can then make sure that no learning outcomes are missed and that learning opportunities are maximised.

Who this unit is for

This unit is for people who train learner driver/riders of all vehicles.

Glossary

Your organisation:	*This is the company you work for or, if you are self employed, the rules you have set for yourself to make sure you comply with relevant legal and licensing requirements.*
Vehicle:	*This covers all powered means of travel, such as cars, motorcycles, vans, etc.*
Driver/rider:	*This includes drivers or riders of all vehicles.*
Learner:	*This term can indicate novice, partly trained, trained or experienced driver/riders, including those who may be adding a licence category.*

Unit 6.2 – Design learning programmes

Performance standards	Knowledge and understanding requirements
You must be able to	You must know and understand
1. confirm that the learner holds a provisional or full licence for the category of the training vehicle	a. the content and principles of the relevant national standard(s) for driving/riding
2. confirm that the learner's eyesight meets licence requirements	b. the requirements of licence acquisition and the content of the practical driving test for the vehicle being used
3. identify the learning needs of the learner, their initial learning status and any special needs, including any need for in-vehicle adaptations	c. the difference between driving, serious and dangerous faults on the practical driving test
4. transfer the learner to an appropriate colleague where their learning needs exceed your competence, such as learners with physical or cognitive disabilities with which you are not familiar, or where you cannot provide a suitably adapted vehicle	d. the requirements of any other formal, post-test assessment of driving competence
	e. the range of prior-learning inputs that can add to the learning process and how they can be featured in the way the learner is taught
5. plan an outline programme that delivers equal opportunities and access to learning, including one-to-one and group-based sessions where suitable	f. the range of special needs that learners might have and their broad implications for driving or riding the training vehicle
6. create lesson plans for each session that outline learning objectives, identify any resources needed and take into account any special needs (such as reduced concentration spans or fatigue due to physical conditions)	g. how cultural and religious factors may affect the options available to support the learning process, such as • inability to attend sessions on particular days of the week • sensitivities about making eye-contact • the belief that it is 'bad manners' to contradict the teacher
7. make sure that any resources in the plan will be available, including e-learning and third-party providers	h. the options available for including non-vehicle-based or third-party learning inputs in the learning programme
	i. best practice tools, techniques, exercises and activities available to support transfer of ownership of the learning process and delivery of desired learning outcomes
	j. the ethical issues involved in the use of psychometric tools
	k. the learning resources available to support driver/rider learning in general and those with special needs in particular

National standard for driver and rider training   www.gov.uk/dvsa/driving-standards

8. include competent third parties, where this will benefit the learner	l. how to draw up learning programmes that cater for different learning styles and needs, including
9. agree roles and responsibilities of any third-party providers, including how they will record and pass on relevant information	• literacy issues • numeracy issues
10. where accompanying driver/riders are involved, specify how they can best support each stage of the programme	• language issues • physical disabilities
11. where applicable, specify how parents, guardians, partners or carers can support learners with physical or cognitive disabilities	• cognitive disabilities m. how to plan routes for on-road training sessions that provide safe, legal and effective learning opportunities
12. specify how you will review learner progress and programme effectiveness	n. how to manage effective working relationships with other providers
	o. the law on accompanying driver/riders
	p. how to maximise the contribution of an accompanying driver or rider to a learning programme
	q. where appropriate, how to foster effective relationships with the parents, guardians, partners or carers of learners with physical or cognitive disabilities
	r. how to monitor and review learning programmes in the light of
	• learners' changing needs
	• learners' progress
	• any formative assessment requirements
	s. how to gather the learners' views of the learning process
	• formally and informally
	• while maintaining confidentiality and trust
	• while remaining within the stated learning objectives
	t. how to manage confidentiality and data security requirements for learning programmes

Role 6 - Deliver driver/rider training programmes

Role 6 Unit 3 – Enable safe and responsible driving/riding

What this unit is about

This unit is about helping and supporting a learner to acquire the skills, knowledge and understanding that they need to drive safely and responsibly throughout their driving career. This means that the unit is not just about teaching a learner to pass a test. Instead, it is about developing the learner's competence and their willingness to continue the learning process beyond their test.

The competences which go to make up this unit are presented in four elements. However, it is important to understand that the first three of these elements represent different aspects, or layers, of a single, integrated, approach; an approach known as 'client-centred learning'*. It is not really possible or meaningful to attempt to demonstrate these competences in isolation.

The fourth element, which is about group-based learning (typically but not always in a classroom environment) shares the 'client-centred' approach. However, it is presented here as a separate element to reflect the fact that some instructors may choose to never work in this environment.

Client-centred learning is not about the learner taking charge of the learning process and deciding what is going to happen. Instead it is about creating a conversation between the learner and the instructor that is based on mutual respect. This approach is based on the idea that people resist taking on new understandings and resist modifying their behaviour if

- the person who is trying to teach them fails to respect and value their idea of who they are

- the person delivering the learning is not seen as 'genuine'

- the person delivering the learning is not seen as having legitimate authority

In the context of learning to drive or ride, the instructor brings to the learning process their hard-earned knowledge, understanding and experience. If they rely simply on telling the learner what they should do they will probably be able to teach them enough to pass their test. However, all the evidence suggests that learners in this sort of relationship do not really change the way they think and quickly forget what they have been taught. There is a better chance of a long-lasting change in understanding and behaviour if the instructor

- presents their knowledge, understanding and experience clearly and effectively

- listens to the learner's reactions to that input

- helps the learner to identify any obstacles to understanding and change

- supports the learner to identify strategies for overcoming those obstacles for themselves

*In this context the phrase 'client-centred' is taken to mean, broadly, the same thing as 'student-centred' or 'learner-centred'.

National standard for driver and rider training   www.gov.uk/dvsa/driving-standards

In this context this unit is not about teaching learners to perform driving or riding tasks in particular ways. While it is reasonable to encourage learners to practise particular methods for performing a given task, because there are clearly explainable benefits to that method, the outcome of the learning process should be that the learner has developed a safe and responsible method which they can apply consistently and reliably; not that they have learnt any one specified method.
This unit contains four elements

      Element 6.3.1 – Create a climate that promotes learning

      Element 6.3.2 – Explain and demonstrate skills and techniques

      Element 6.3.3 – Coach

      Element 6.3.4 – Facilitate group-based learning

Who this unit is for

This unit is for people who train learner driver/riders of all vehicles.

Glossary

Your organisation:	*This is the company you work for or, if you are self employed, the rules you have set for yourself to make sure you comply with relevant legal and licensing requirements.*
Vehicle:	*This covers all powered means of travel, such as cars, motorcycles, vans, etc.*
Driver/rider:	*This includes drivers or riders of all vehicles.*
Learner:	*This term can indicate novice, partly trained, trained or experienced driver/riders, including those who may be adding a licence category.*

Unit 6.3 – Enable safe and responsible driving/riding

Element 6.3.1 – Create a climate that promotes learning

About this element

This element is about creating a relationship with the learner, and a context for their learning, that helps them to take ownership of their learning process. It is the foundation on which the next two elements are built.

This approach is based on the understanding that learners who

- are not engaged by the training

- just receive information

are less well equipped to deal with the wide range of challenges they will meet, when they drive independently, than those who are supported to be active learners.

The element is also about ensuring that every learner has access to the same learning opportunities and is treated with equal respect.

Performance standards	Knowledge and understanding requirements
You must be able to	You must know and understand
1. establish an effective verbal and/or non-verbal communications strategy that	a. how to ensure and improve good verbal and/or non-verbal communication, such as by
• is free from discrimination	• using good eye-contact (where this is culturally acceptable)
• does not exploit the learner	• using consistent language
• does not collude with risky behaviour or attitudes	• breaking things into manageable pieces
2. make sure the learner fully understands the objectives, structure and formal assessment requirements of the programme	• using graphics, pictures and other visual aids to reinforce your words
3. explain how you expect to work with the learner and how you expect them to work with you	b. the content and principles of the relevant national standard for driving/riding
4. make sure the learner understands what other opportunities, methods and resources are available and how these can be included in their overall learning process	c. the evidence that indicates that an active and lifelong approach to learning reduces the risk of crashes and the long-term cost of driving

5. where appropriate, explain how parents, guardians, partners or carers can support learners with physical or cognitive disabilities

6. where a driver accompanies the learner on private practice, explain how they can be most effective in supporting the learner

7. explain how you intend to monitor and review the learner's progress during the programme

8. agree the details of the learning plan with the learner

- within the constraints of the overall programme

- with the understanding that you may work with the learner to agree changes if required

d. how to set clear guidelines for acceptable behaviour within the learning environment

e. the effect of your own assumptions about particular groups within society on your ability to deliver effective learning

f. the role of 'individual learning plans' and similar models for agreeing ways forward within learning programmes

g. how to identify and deal with possible barriers to learning and achievement, including

- delivery methods

- times

- location

- lack of support for people with special needs

- lack of facilities

h. how to explain the objectives and structure of a learning programme, and your choice of methods, in a way that is appropriate for each learner

i. how to include accompanying driver/riders in the learning process in a way that reinforces learning outcomes

j. the scope for flexibility within the programme

k. the credibility of the licence acquisition process with key stakeholders such as parents or employers

l. the credibility of post-test assessments of driving competence with key stakeholders such as parents or employers

m. external influences on the learner's attitude to the learning process, such as economic factors and peer pressure

Unit 6.3 – Enable safe and responsible driving/riding

Element 6.3.2 - Explain and demonstrate skills and techniques

---

About this element

Within the learner-centred approach, there is a legitimate role for well delivered explanation and demonstration. This element sets out the standards for this. Instructors should be able to provide clear, realistic and reliable demonstrations of how to apply practical skills – both stationary and moving. They should be able to explain what they are doing and why they are doing it. Having provided such demonstrations, they should then be able to support the learner in practising the skills and give them feedback.

The element assumes that the process of learning practical skills is helped if the learner understands the reasons why a particular skill is necessary.

Performance standards	Knowledge and understanding requirements
You must be able to	You must know and understand
1. select suitable locations for delivering demonstrations	a. how to deliver an explanation or demonstration so that the learner gains the maximum learning, taking into account different learning styles
2. provide timely and appropriate explanations and demonstrations of the skills and techniques required to drive or ride a vehicle safely and responsibly, including the use of adaptations where fitted	b. how to make sure that the learner understands the purpose and content of any explanation or demonstration
3. encourage learners to ask questions and, where necessary, repeat or alter your answer so that they understand	c. how to assess whether a location is suitable for the demonstration of a skill or technique
4. make sure that the learner understands any theory that links to on-road application of the skill or technique being taught	d. that while frequent explanations and demonstrations can be supportive for some learners, for others this may be demotivating e. how to overcome the limitations of the in-vehicle environment*
5. make sure that learners have enough opportunities to practise the skill demonstrated	f. how to provide explanations and demonstrations in practical driving skills while stationary
6. give feedback to learners that helps	

---

* Those training motorcycle or moped riders face particular challenges when delivering on-road training. In this context this element should be taken to include the use of two-way radio and any other similar devices that enable machine to machine communication.

them identify, understand and overcome obstacles to competent application of skills 7. where possible, encourage and help learners to practise skills in a structured way, outside the formal learning environment	g. how to carry out a moving vehicle demonstration while keeping full control of the vehicle h. how to provide a verbal explanation of what you are doing while carrying out a moving vehicle demonstration * i. the content of the Highway Code and the requirements of the licence acquisition theory test j. the importance of moving the use of vehicle controls, and other practical skills, from active effort to implicit or procedural memory as quickly as possible k. how to check the learner's understanding and progress l. how to give formative feedback

* In this unit the ability to provide an explanation of what you are doing as you are doing it is considered to be a level 3 competence. The more complex process of 'commentary driving' is considered to be a level 4 competence.

Unit 6.3 – Enable safe and responsible driving/riding

Element 6.3.3 – Coach

About this element

This element is about engaging in a conversation with the learner to help them identify obstacles to learning and strategies for overcoming those obstacles.

Note: It is unlikely that a learner will be willing to engage in this process if a secure grounding has not been established in element 6.3.1.

Performance standards	Knowledge and understanding requirements
You must be able to	You must know and understand
1. listen to what the learner tells you about the obstacles they experience that prevent them from applying • practical driving skills • their understanding of theory 2. help the learner to come up with strategies for overcoming obstacles 3. work with the learner to help them reflect on • their experience of the learning programme • your feedback • the feedback of other providers 4. work with the learner to identify obstacles to their ownership of the learning process and work out strategies for overcoming those obstacles 5. transfer the balance of responsibility for their learning process to the learner as soon as they are ready to take it 6. at all times, exercise your responsibility for the safety of yourself, the learner and other road users 7. work with the learner to agree when they are ready for formal assessment of driving competence	a. how to use a range of learner-centred techniques to help the learner identify and overcome barriers to achievement of learning goals b. how to use a range of learner-centred techniques to encourage the learner to join-up their understanding of practice and theory and of different parts of theory c. how to use a range of learner-centred techniques to support the transfer of ownership of the learning process to the learner d. the impact of your own willingness to transfer ownership of the learning process e. the importance of providing regular formative feedback f. how to use learner-centred techniques while putting your responsibility for safety in the learning environment first

8. accompany the learner to formal assessments when appropriate

9. work with the learner to help them

- reflect on their experience of assessment

- reflect on examiner feedback

- identify strategies for overcoming problems when they have failed an assessment

Unit 6.3 – Enable safe and responsible driving/riding

Element 6.3.4 – Facilitate group-based learning

About this element

This element shares the broad objectives of elements 6.3.1 – 6.3.3; creating a suitable learning environment, providing inputs based on expertise and working with the learner to identify obstacles to learning and strategies for overcoming those obstacles. It recognises that delivering these objectives when working with a group of learners presents extra challenges and barriers to learning. This calls for extra competences.

Performance standards

You must be able to

1. make sure all learners feel comfortable and able to express their views and concerns

2. encourage all learners to ask questions and, where necessary, modify your delivery to ensure understanding

3. make sure learners understand the purpose, processes and intended outcomes of each group activity, and how it links to the rest of their learning programme

4. support all learners to take an active part in learning activities

5. make sure individual behaviours or group dynamics do not isolate individuals or distract from the desired learning outcomes

6. make sure you do not collude with inappropriate attitudes to other group members or to road safety

Knowledge and understanding requirements

You must know and understand

a. how to make sure learners feel

- at their ease within the group

- safe

- able to take an active part in the learning process

b. how to use a range of learning activities that involve all members of the group so that they gain the maximum learning benefit

c. how to use learner-centred techniques to help individuals

- identify obstacles to engagement with the learning process

- devise strategies for overcoming obstacles

d. the potential effect of peer group assumptions on the behaviour of learners

e. the risk of group dynamics being dominated by sub-groups

f. how to interrupt individual behaviours or group dynamics which have the effect of excluding individuals or sub-groups

g. the risk of unconsciously colluding with inappropriate behaviours or attitudes

h. the risk of being diverted from intended learning outcomes by group dynamics

National standard for driver and rider training   www.gov.uk/dvsa/driving-standards

7. promptly and clearly interrupt behaviour that is

- discriminatory

- oppressive

- preventing any individual from benefiting from the learning experience whether by other learners or by colleagues

8. monitor the progress of individuals and provide feedback to the learner and other providers

i. how to identify opportunities to increase learning that arise in the group, and how to adapt presentations to support that process

j. how to check an individual's understanding and progress within a group

k. how to give feedback in a group and on a one-to-one basis

l. how to provide feedback on individual learner progress to other training providers

Role 6 - Deliver driver/rider training programmes

Role 6 Unit 4 – Manage risk to instructor, learner and third parties

What this unit is about

This unit is about actively managing the risks that can arise while delivering driver/rider training and ensuring, as far as is within your control, the health and safety of all involved.
This unit contains three elements

Element 6.4.1 – Manage the on-road environment to minimise risk

Element 6.4.2 – Manage the risk of violence in the learning environment

Element 6.4.3 – Manage health and safety in the classroom environment

Who this unit is for

This unit is for people who train learner driver/riders of all vehicles.

Glossary

Your organisation:	*This is the company you work for or, if you are self employed, the rules you have set for yourself to make sure you comply with relevant legal and licensing requirements.*
Vehicle:	*This covers all powered means of travel, such as cars, motorcycles, vans, etc.*
Driver/rider:	*This includes drivers or riders of all vehicles.*
Learner:	*This term can indicate novice, partly trained, trained or experienced driver/riders, including those who may be adding a licence category.*
Classroom:	*An enclosed learning space in which formal training is regularly delivered.*

Unit 6.4 – Manage risk to instructor, learner and third parties

Element 6.4.1 – Manage the on-road environment to minimise risk

About this element

This element addresses those risks that can arise in an on-road training session. It assumes that learners will always be expected to take their share of responsibility for the management of risk, while recognising that their competence to take that responsibility will change over the period of their training. It also recognises that correctly understanding the nature of the risks that arise during a training session is central to a learner's ability to assess and respond to risk when they drive/ride independently.

Performance standards	Knowledge and understanding requirements
You must be able to	You must know and understand
1. make sure you are fit to teach, and take suitable action if you are not	a. the importance of being fit to teach and able to manage the safety of the lesson effectively
2. take reasonable steps to make sure the learner is fit to start the session, and take suitable action if they are not fit	b. the signs that a learner's fitness to be trained may be impaired by
3. make sure the learner fully understands how you will share with them the responsibility for	• alcohol
• their safety	• illegal or controlled substances
• your safety	• over-the-counter or prescription medicines
• the safety of other road users	c. the signs that a learner may be suffering from a physical or psychological condition that makes them unfit to be trained, including conditions that they are
4. give clear and timely instructions (such as when and where to start, stop or turn), make sure that the learner understands your instructions and, if they do not, modify your instructions accordingly	• unaware of
	• trying to hide
5. ensure that any ancillary equipment used in a lesson is working properly	d. what to do if you believe a learner
	• is temporarily unfit to be trained
	• has a permanent physical or psychological condition that they have not revealed
	e. how far you are responsible for the health and safety of yourself and others in the on-road learning environment

6. ensure the learner knows to respond to the actual situation on the road ahead if a satellite navigation system stops working or provides confusing guidance

7. explain when and how you may use verbal or physical interventions to ensure safety

8. continue to scan the environment and assess hazards while observing the learner and providing training inputs

9. take suitable and timely action where you

- identify a hazard that the learner does not appear to be aware of

- believe the learner is unable to respond safely to a hazard

10. use 'client-centred' techniques to make sure the learner is better equipped to deal with such hazards in the future

11. take suitable and timely action, including stopping the session, where the learner becomes unfit to continue or behaves in a way that places you, the learner or third parties at unacceptable risk

12. comply with any requirement to record details of situations in which specific risks arise

13. where the learner has driven/ridden before but they are new to you, verify their learning status using an assessment drive/ride, where appropriate

14. when delivering compulsory basic training (CBT) to learner riders, make a reasonable assessment of their ability to ride safely on the road

f. how far the learner is responsible for health and safety in the on-road learning environment*

g. that as a supervising driver you are considered to be in control of the vehicle and learner driver, and must obey the rules of the road as if you were driving the vehicle yourself (for example, you must not use a mobile phone or be under the influence of alcohol whilst supervising a learner)

h. how to safely integrate the use of satellite navigation systems into an on-road lesson and the sorts of problems that drivers can have when using them

i. how you can take action, safely, and how this depends on the type of training vehicle**

j. where applicable, how to operate dual-controls

k. how to give feedback about risk-related issues so that you motivate and help the learner to change their behaviour without increasing fear-based responses

l. what to do if a learner becomes unfit to continue the session

m. how to promptly interrupt deliberate behaviour that places the instructor, learner or third parties at risk

n. the instructor's right to interrupt or stop sessions where an unacceptable risk arises

o. how to record incidents in which a risk situation arises

p. the impact of your own level of competence and attitudes to risk on your ability to minimise risk

q. the importance of demonstrating consistent attitudes to the management of risk to make

* It is particularly important to understand how the balance of the responsibility may vary between vehicles. An instructor clearly has far less ability to act in the context of category A/M machines than in vehicles where they can take more direct control.
** This understanding is particularly important for category A/M vehicles where the only intervention available is usually through two-way radio. In this context a sudden alarm may, in itself, distract the learner.

	sure that formal messages being given in the learning programme are not undermined
	r. how to conduct a safe assessment drive/ride

Unit 6.4 – Manage risk to instructor, learner and third parties

Element 6.4.2 – Manage the risk of violence in the learning environment

---

About this element

The Health and Safety Executive notes that

"People who deal directly with the public may face aggressive or violent behaviour. They may be sworn at, threatened or even attacked."

This unit is about taking steps to protect yourself, and learners, from aggressive or violent behaviour, whether from other learners or third parties. The 'Management of Health and Safety at Work Regulations 1999' say that employers must assess the risks to employees and make arrangements for their health and safety by effective

- planning

- organisation

- control

- monitoring and review

Therefore, it is assumed that any training organisation will have policies and guidance on how to deal with aggressive or violent behaviour. It is important that instructors understand what actions they can take to protect themselves and others, both to make sure that they are safe and that they comply with legal requirements and limits.

Performance standards	Knowledge and understanding requirements
You must be able to	You must know and understand
1. implement and comply with your organisation's policy and procedures for protecting staff from the risk of violence at work	a. your legal responsibility to your well-being, safety and health in the workplace as set out in the relevant legislation for Health and Safety at Work
2. implement and comply with your organisation's policy and procedures for protecting learners from the risk of violence during sessions	b. the extent and limits of your obligation to protect learners from the risk of physical or verbal violence during sessions
3. manage verbally or physically aggressive behaviour in ways that are consistent with best practice and legal requirements	

4. take appropriate and timely action, inline with your organisation's policy and procedures, including

- stopping the session

- calling for assistance

- leaving the learning space

if a learner's behaviour puts you or others at risk

5. report details of any situation in which an actual or potential risk of aggressive or violent behaviour arises, in line with your organisation's policy and procedures

c. your organisation's policy and procedures for the management of violence in the learning environment including

- stopping sessions

- summoning assistance

- leaving the learning space

and how they apply to your role and level of competence

d. how to interpret body language, and the importance of acknowledging other people's personal space

e. the impact of your own level of competence and attitudes and how they may trigger aggressive or violent responses

f. the limits to your ability to protect yourself in potentially violent situations

g. when and how you can safely interrupt behaviour which appears likely to result in violence

h. how to record incidents in which a risk situation arises

i. the importance of demonstrating consistent attitudes and behaviours in the management of violence in the learning environment so that messages being given in the overall learning programme are not undermined

Unit 6.4 – Manage risk to instructor, learner and third parties

Element 6.4.3 - Manage health and safety in the classroom environment

---

About this element

This element is about those particular health and safety issues that arise when using enclosed premises for the delivery of any part of the training process, in particular where groups of learners are involved. It assumes that the risk of violence in the classroom is covered in 6.4.2.

Performance standards	Knowledge and understanding requirements
You must be able to	You must know and understand
1. implement and follow general health and safety procedures and requirements for the delivery of services to the public	a. the extent and limits of your responsibility for learners as set out in the relevant Health and Safety at Work legislation
2. implement and follow any specific health and safety procedures and requirements that apply in the buildings you are using	b. the application of health and safety regulations in any enclosed premises
3. make sure that learners understand the operation of health and safety and emergency procedures that apply in any enclosed premises you are using	c. the content of your organisation's health and safety policy and procedures and how they apply to your role and responsibilities
4. in the event of an emergency, carry out your responsibilities as set out in your organisation's policy and procedures	d. the operation of fire alarm and emergency evacuation procedures
5. report details of any actual or potential health and safety risks that arise, in line with your organisation's policy and procedures	e. the importance of remaining alert to health and safety issues at all times
	f. the importance of demonstrating consistent attitudes and behaviours in the management of health and safety risks so that messages being given in the overall learning programme are not undermined

National standard for driver and rider training
www.gov.uk/dvsa/driving-standards

Role 6 - Deliver driver/rider training programmes

Role 6 Unit 5 - Evaluate and develop your knowledge, understanding and skills in the driver/rider training industry

What this unit is about

This unit is about evaluating your own performance against the established and evolving requirements of your role, identifying where there are opportunities for improvement and taking action to respond to those opportunities.

It is recognised that many organisations will have a formal personal development process in place with which an employed instructor will be expected to comply. However, beyond this requirement, any competent instructor should be able to demonstrate that they are actively involved in maintaining and continuously improving their skills, knowledge and understanding whether they are employed or self-employed.

Who this unit is for

This unit is for people who train learner driver/riders of all vehicles.

Glossary

Your organisation:	*This is the company you work for or, if you are self employed, the rules you have set for yourself to make sure you comply with relevant legal and licensing requirements.*
Vehicle:	*This covers all powered means of travel, such as cars, motorcycles, vans, etc.*
Driver/rider:	*This includes drivers or riders of all vehicles.*
Learner:	*This term can indicate novice, partly trained, trained or experienced driver/riders, including those who may be adding a licence category.*

National standard for driver and rider training
www.gov.uk/dvsa/driving-standards

Unit 6.5 - Evaluate and develop your knowledge, understanding and skills in the driver/rider training industry

Performance standards	Knowledge and understanding requirements
You must be able to	You must know and understand
1. identify the skills, knowledge and understanding needed for your role and evaluate your own capabilities and performance against these	a. the personal and professional benefits of evaluating and developing your knowledge, understanding and skills
2. evaluate your working practices against relevant organisational and legal requirements	b. the requirements of the relevant national standard(s) for driving/riding
3. keep up to date with training industry issues and recognise when changes in the industry mean that you need to update your knowledge, skills and understanding	c. the requirements of the 'National standard for driver and rider training'
4. actively make use of all sources of feedback, such as	d. the DVSA's standards check requirements, and how they will be assessed
• performance records of previous learners • feedback from line managers	e. any regulatory requirements for continuing professional development
• feedback from colleagues or other professionals	f. the performance and knowledge requirements of any other body by which you are employed
to identify gaps in your knowledge, skills or understanding	g. how to obtain feedback on your performance in a non-defensive way
5. set out objectives for the ongoing development of your knowledge, skills and understanding	h. current developments in driver/rider training practice
	i. how to evaluate your own performance against requirements
6. identify training or development opportunities that will help you update or close any gaps in your knowledge, skills and understanding	j. how to recognise where gaps in your skills, knowledge or understanding are affecting your performance
7. keep a reflective log so that you can evaluate the outcome of your professional development activities	k. the opportunities for formal and informal professional development available through your employers or other providers
8. comply with any organisational requirements to plan and record your training and development activities and to evaluate the benefits of any training you undertake	l. how to record and evaluate your professional practice in a reflective log
	m. how to build an achievable development plan and set yourself realistic objectives and priorities
	n. how to monitor your performance against your development plans

National standard for driver and rider training   www.gov.uk/dvsa/driving-standards

Role 6 - Deliver driver/rider training programmes

Unit 6.6 – Develop and use a programme of role play for trainee instructors

What this unit is about

This unit is about developing and implementing a programme of role play for those training to be driving or riding instructors. The role play will help trainee instructors to learn how to deal with situations that they may come across with their learners.

You will know when role play is appropriate to use as a training method, and be aware of the strengths and limitations of its use. You will be able to brief the trainee instructor and undertake a variety of roles yourself as a trainer. You will be able to make sure the role play develops the trainee instructor's confidence by using accurate and supportive feedback. You will know when to close the role play and be able to help the trainee instructor to understand the learning achieved.

You will appreciate the importance of, and need to comply with, relevant health and safety practices and road traffic legislation in all role play activity.

This unit contains two elements

Element 6.6.1 – Develop a programme of role play

Element 6.6.2 – Implement a programme of role play

Who this unit is for

This unit is for people who train learner driver/riders of all vehicles.

National standard for driver and rider training   www.gov.uk/dvsa/driving-standards

Glossary

Your organisation: This is the company you work for or, if you are self employed, the rules you have set for yourself to make sure you comply with relevant legal and licensing requirements.

Vehicle: This covers all powered means of travel, such as cars, motorcycles, vans, etc.

Driver/rider: This includes drivers or riders of all vehicles.

Learner: This term can indicate novice, partly trained, trained or experienced driver/riders, including those who may be adding a licence category.

Fault: This includes any area of a learner's driving or riding that needs development.

Simulation: Committing (or appearing to commit) driving or riding faults. Displaying development needs.

Role play: This consists of both portraying a character and simulating faults/development needs. The character portrayal supports the simulation.

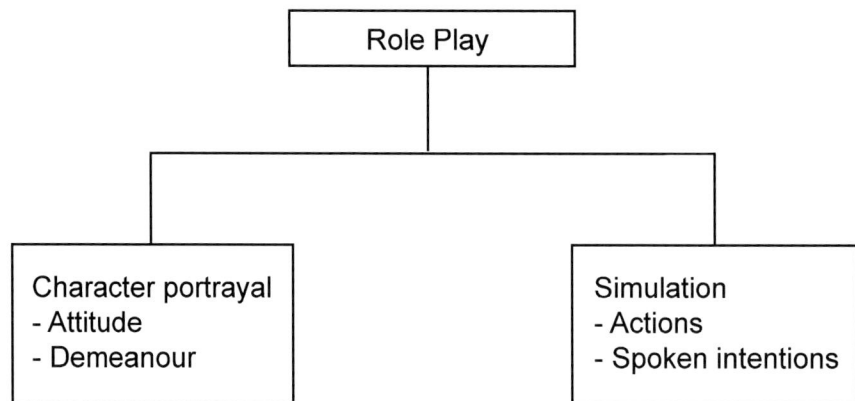

```
                    ┌─────────────┐
                    │  Role Play  │
                    └──────┬──────┘
          ┌────────────────┴────────────────┐
┌───────────────────────┐         ┌───────────────────────┐
│ Character portrayal    │         │ Simulation            │
│ - Attitude             │         │ - Actions             │
│ - Demeanour            │         │ - Spoken intentions   │
└───────────────────────┘         └───────────────────────┘
```

National standard for driver and rider training   www.gov.uk/dvsa/driving-standards

Unit 6.6 – Develop and use a programme of role play for trainee instructors

Element 6.6.1 – Develop a programme of role play

About this element

This element is about developing a realistic programme of role play to be used with trainee instructors.

Performance standards	Knowledge and understanding requirements
You must be able to	You must know and understand
1. identify when role play could be an effective training activity	a. the strengths and limitations of role play
2. design role play activities that are realistic, reliable and credible	b. how to develop role play situations that meet the needs of the trainee instructor
3. make sure that the role play is relevant to the needs of trainee instructors	c. when the use of role play is helpful, and when to use other methods
4. define learning outcomes for each role play situation	d. the types of faults and style of driving or riding common to various types of learners
5. plan routes that are suitable for each role play situation	e. for which situations role play is not a safe training method
6. plan simulation that makes sure that you, the trainee instructor and other road users are not put at risk	

Unit 6.6 – Develop and use a programme of role play for trainee instructors

Element 6.6.2 – Use a programme of role play

About this element

This element is about using the programme of role play with trainee instructors, and managing the role play effectively and safely.

Performance standards

You must be able to

1. make sure that the instructor is briefed on the learning outcome(s) of the role play

2. brief the trainee instructor on how you will manage the role play, for example how you will communicate with them during the role play and how you will give feedback

3. make sure the trainee instructor knows when you are in or out of role

4. make sure that your behaviour is consistent with the brief you have given to the trainee instructor

5. stay in role while the role play is meeting the learning outcome(s) and close the role play when it is not meeting the learning outcome(s)

6. maintain the focus of the role play on the learning outcome(s)

7. scan the driving space and plan your driving or riding so that you have all-round awareness at all times

8. make sure that safe practices are followed while in role, such as

   - verbal simulation of high risk faults where possible

   - threatening unsafe manoeuvres without actually making the manoeuvre

   - portrayal of high risk attitudes that act as a barrier to safe and responsible driving or riding, where appropriate

Knowledge and understanding requirements

You must know and understand

a. how to give the trainee instructor a brief on the purpose of and arrangements for the role play

b. the importance of supporting the brief by

   - communicating in a way that does not alter the trainee instructor's perception of you as a learner

   - driving or riding in a way that does not alter the trainee instructor's perception of you as a learner

   - reacting realistically to the trainee instructor's responses

c. how to make it clear when role play begins and ends, and recognise when, to end the role play

d. techniques for scanning the driving space and planning your driving or riding whilst also observing the trainee instructor

e. the safe practices and legislation relevant to the role play, and

   - that no faults can be committed that contravene the rules of the road or affect other road users

   - that no faults that involve vulnerable road users should be committed

   - how to simulate risky attitudes

   - what types of faults you can simulate verbally